THE DIGITAL FUTURE OF CURRENCIES

FUTURE OF CURRENCIES

A look into how digital currencies will command the future of finance

SIVACHANDRAN PAZHANI

INDIA · SINGAPORE · MALAYSIA

Notion Press

Old No. 38, New No. 6
McNichols Road, Chetpet
Chennai - 600 031

First Published by Notion Press 2020
Copyright © Sivachandran Pazhani 2020
All Rights Reserved.

ISBN 978-1-64899-738-9

Disclaimer

No part of this eBook can be transmitted or reproduced in any form, including print, electronic, photocopying, scanning, mechanical, or recording without prior written permission from the author.

This is a work of creative nonfiction. The events are portrayed to the best of the author's memories. While all the stories in this book are true, some names and identifying details have been changed to protect the privacy of the people involved.

This e-book has been written for information purposes only. Every effort has been made to make this eBook as complete and accurate as possible. However, there may be mistakes in typography or content. Also, this e-book provides information only up to the publishing date, so it may not include some information about the author's life.

The purpose of this eBook is to *educate and inform* others going through difficult times. The author and the publisher do not warrant that the information contained in this e-book is fully complete and shall not be responsible for any errors or omissions. The author and publisher shall have neither liability nor responsibility to any person or entity with respect to any loss or damage caused or alleged to be caused directly or indirectly by this e-book.

Contents

Introduction

The concept and value of money have changed with the passage of time. Money itself has evolved with time, and is now at a point where it is ready for further progress.

Throughout the history of money, we have always perceived and associated value with the terms and numbers used to define currency. Money has also significantly developed from something that you can both touch and use to something that you just have an abstract idea of.

However, regardless of how the tangible aspects of money have progressed, the value we associate with money in our minds has always been and will be the same. The abstract concept of the value associated with money eventually brings us to the next major step in the ladder towards progression in currency; digital currency.

Similar to all previous forms of money, digital currencies are the future because of how people believe in them and associate value with them. In this book we look at and dissect the future of money in relation to digital currencies. The future is here and it is time we financially prepared ourselves for it.

Chapter 1

Digital Currencies and Where We Stand Today

This chapter will look into the major digital currencies of today and where they stand.

Both 2017 and 2018 saw tremendous growth in the world of digital currencies. Crypto currencies from over the world saw a defining rise in their market cap and value. While some of the early gains made during these years have been corrected, it is time we realize that digital currencies are here and aren't going anywhere anytime soon.

In this chapter we study some of the top performing digital currencies the world over and what makes these currencies popular among the masses.

Bitcoin (BTC)

The first of our top 10 crypto currencies on the list is Bitcoin. Bitcoin was the first ever crypto currency to be launched in 2008. The currency was created online by a person who likes being referred to as Satoshi Nakamoto. Nakamoto has made no public or private appearances after the release of bitcoin and we don't have any idea who she or he could be. For all we know, Nakamoto could be a pseudonym for multiple different developers working under the same umbrella.

Bitcoin is based on the distributed ledger technology of blockchain and eliminates the need for centralized intermediaries like credit card companies and banks etc. Your electronic payments are secured through blockchain, which is just as secure as the solutions provided by any other intermediary.

You can pay 1 BTC to a friend without involving your bank or any other regulated agency for that matter. The Blockchain comes with its own pros and cons, but it is trusted to be secure and effective by users all over the world.

Bitcoin Pros

- One of the reasons we are counting BTC to be the most established cryptocurrency in the world is because it is the oldest one going around. Also, BTC comes with a growing community of investors and developers backing it to achieve further growth.
- It is easy for investors to purchase and deal in BTC. The currency is supported by and adopted in the mainstream economy. Transactions through bitcoins are supported by all major exchanges and wallets. Platforms like Microsoft, Overstock and Bloomberg have also started accepting payments made through bitcoin.

Ethereum

Ethereum is the second most popular digital or crypto currency after Bitcoin and was created back in 2015. The currency was created by VitalikButerin and is a lot more than just a simple digital currency.

Those who haven't studied Ethereum and don't know much about the full spectrum of services provided by them would be surprised to know that Ethereum is basically a blockchain platform for developing smart contracts and decentralized applications. Ether is conveniently used as the native digital currency option on all transactions on the Ethereumblockchain.

Ethereum differs from other digital currencies, because it gives developers an opportunity to develop their own coded blockchain. You can start building your preferred project/application on Ethereum'sblockchain. Hence, ethereum is more than just a simple digital currency; it is an entire blockchain platform.

Pros of Ethereum

- Ethereum provides a decent platform for new digital currencies to see the light of day and offer Initial Coin Offerings in the market.
- Ethereum has a rapid transaction speed. Recent measures specify that they are the fastest in the bunch.
- Ethereum is good for building and executing smart contracts. If you're unaware of them, smart contracts are basically agreements coded on the blockchain. These agreements execute themselves after the fulfillment of certain pre-set conditions.

Ripple

Ripple is a solution oriented digital currency, which was formed with the sole purpose of finding a solution to the constant problem of international transactions. When

Ripple was founded in 2012, the founders wanted to provide a convenient and an easy setup for international payment transfers. Out of the 100 billion Ripple coins existing today, 50 billion are exclusively owned and operated by Ripple Labs, the company running and managing Ripple. This entire approach is different from the other digital currencies on the list. No other currency has one single, operating entity holding a majority of the shares in the market.

Pros of Ripple

- An international money transfer usually takes months to actualize. With the use of Ripple, you can manage such money transfers within a matter of seconds. The fee charged by Ripple is also considerably lower than what is charged by other financial institutions and crypto currencies.
- Ripple targets just one part of the money market – financial payments, and does a good job at it.
- Ripple is being tested out by other services the world over.

EOS

EOS is a direct competitor to NEO and Ethereum when it comes to the scope of the services they provide. The ICO for EOS was launched in June of 2017, and the company has made giant leaps ever since.

Created by Dan Larimer, the EOS platform was created with the sole purpose of helping developers build smart contracts and decentralized applications through the security of the block chain. The EOS platform was made to ramp up the current standards in technology and add innovation within the blockchain setup.

Pros of EOS

- Developers working on EOS consider the platform to be more reliable and safer than Ethereum because of the advance mechanisms used here. The platform comes with Byzantine Fault Tolerance and Delegated Proof of Stake technology. Transactions are verified at the rate of 10,000 – 100,000 transactions per second.
- EOS supports multiple languages including C++
- The team behind EOS is experienced and has their future yet to come

Bitcoin Cash

As the name for BCH or Bitcoin Cash itself suggests, this digital currency was formed from the existing Bitcoin in 2016. The developers behind Bitcoin were unable to reach a decision on the changes required in the code for bitcoin. When the confusion became widespread, developers decided to fork the crypto and form a new digital currency by the name of Bitcoin Cash.

A crypto fork is when a new digital currency is formed from an old one. Parent currencies keep all of their existing features, while the newly formed currency goes through technological improvements.

Pros of Bitcoin Cash

- The block size of Bitcoin Cash is greater than the block size for Bitcoin. Bitcoin has a block size of

1 MB, while BTH has a block size of 8 MBs. This makes Bitcoin Cash even faster than Bitcoin.

- Bitcoin Cash has a transaction fee of $0.067, which is less than the $1.8 charged by BTC.

By now you know the top 5 digital currencies in the world today, and the positive attributes that set them apart from the rest. You are now prepared to study the progression of digital currencies in the next chapter, with special focus on how digital currencies reached the stage they are at currently.

Chapter 2

A Tale of Progression

In this chapter we will study the progression of digital currencies from when they started until today.

Digital currencies across the globe shocked investors and hit front page headlines during their surprising rise in price during 2017 and early 2018. The world had had digital currencies for around a decade in 2018, but these currencies made it to the front pages during that year.

Bitcoin first came into being during 2008. The roots for the technology go even further back. Bitcoin has miraculously grown from the day it was launched to what it is now. If you had invested just $1,000 in bitcoin when it was first launched, you would have had the opportunity to earn over $37 million from the meager investment during the peak in 2017.

Being humans, we learn from history and implement the knowledge in our day to day lives. The one thing that we have learnt from history is that we are doomed to repeat our mistakes if we don't learn from them and abstain from them.

To help you understand how digital currencies have progressed and where they stand today, we take a short look at the history of digital currencies from when the work first started on Bitcoin.

1998 – 2008 Pre-Bitcoin Years

Bitcoin is known to mankind as the first developed digital currency in our entire history. While Bitcoin or BTC was launched on the blockchainin 2008, work on it had started well in advance. Technological wonders like Bitcoin and the blockchain are not created overnight, which is why work is started on them well in advance.

While work on Bitcoin was in progress, we saw the launch of two other online currencies with secured ledgers. B-Money and Bit Gold tried their luck on the online world, but without any success. Besides the issues with encryption, the public reaction to these currencies was also quite lukewarm.

2008 – Enter Mr. Nakamoto

It was in 2008 that a paper called Bitcoin – A Peer to Peer Electronic Cash System was mysteriously posted on a mailing list discussion for cryptography. The paper contained content that had not previously been discussed in the social circles of cryptography. The paper is believed to have been posted by a certain someone calling themselves Satoshi Nakamoto. Nakamoto has since been considered the founder of Bitcoin, but the identity of the person remains a mystery. Some experts studying the case believe that Nakamoto was a pseudonym for a group of cryptographers and developers working on the concept of Bitcoin behind the scenes.

2009 – The Start of Bitcoin

It was during 2019 that the bitcoin network was first made open for the public to access and own. Bitcoin mining was also introduced during the same period. With the process of Bitcoin mining, individuals could own personal mining machines and create new coins for the digital currency. All transactions and new coins are recorded and verified on the blockchain.

The process was new and innovative, which is why it took some time for everyone to catch up with it. However, people who invested in Bitcoin during that period and stuck with their investment have had the biggest benefit from the digital currency.

2010 – Bitcoin is Assigned a Value

During the first few years, Bitcoin was just primarily mined and not traded. The digital currency was not exchanged between individuals and it wasn't used as a source of buying other items. However, it was in 2010 that a monetary value was assigned to Bitcoins, when someone decided to sell the coins they owned.

Private investors believe that the first transaction was when someone swapped 10,000 bitcoins to buy two pizzas. Had the investor stuck with their investment, the 10,000 Bitcoins would be worth over $100 million today.

2011 – Rivals Emerge

As Bitcoin increased in popularity, the potential in digital currencies dawned upon multiple users. Developers and investors realized just how much potential was present in the encrypted and decentralized world of digital currencies.

It was around 2011 that the first competitors for Bitcoin started emerging. These new competitors were known as altcoins, because they copied the structure and design of Bitcoin and worked on it to offer some additional benefits as well.

Some of the new altcoins to appear in the market included Litecoin and Namecoin. Some of the earlier competitors went on to achieve success, while others faced complications. However, the rate at which new alternatives came into the market kept increasing. We have over 1,000 digital currencies in the world today, with new ones appearing left, right and center.

2013 also saw a significant fall in the price of Bitcoins. Prices hit $1,000 for the first time, but they eventually started declining when investors showed heightened interest. People who invested during this period faced losses, as the price fell down to $300.

2014 – Scams and Thefts

Unsurprisingly, a growing market as big as the one for digital currencies, was host to scams and thefts from a wide number of scammers as well. The biggest scam came to light in 2014, when Mt. Gox went offline. Mt. Gox was the largest Bitcoin exchange back then and 850,000 Bitcoins were stolen in the process.

Investigations are underway to get to the bottom of the scandal, but no progress was made. The stolen bitcoins were valued at $450 million dollars in 2014. However, according to today's valuation, the coins would be valued at $4.4 billion.

2016 – ICOs and Ethereum

2016 was the wonder year for crypto currencies, as there was a sudden rise in the number of Initial Coin Offerings.

The only crypto currency that has come close to stealing Bitcoin's oomph and thunder, Ethereum saw considerable success during this year.

Ethereum's arrival and popularity aided the process of Initial Coin Offerings. Through the secure and encrypted platform provided by etherium, investors could get funding for their new crypto currency ventures. The SEC warned citizens of the United States that ICOs could be Ponzi Schemes and citizens should look after themselves.

2017 – Bitcoin Crosses $10,000

Bitcoin crossed the barrier of $10,000 for the first time in 2017. The market cap for all crypto currencies rose exponentially during this period and defined the $300 bn cap that was achieved. Bitcoin eventually went on to achieve its highest recorded value of over $17,000. The market did drop down, but a peak was hit and the public was involved now.

2019 and 2020 – Talks of Regulation and Digital Fiat Currencies

There have been multiple talks of regulating crypto currencies during the last two years. Some countries have also shown interest in building digital versions of their fiat currencies. The peak of 2017-18 had done its job. Lawmakers and investors across the world knew that digital currencies were here to stay.

Chapter 3

What the Future Looks Like

This chapter will study the future of currencies and the massive role played by digital currencies in it.

As we expect you to be well aware of by now, a cryptocurrency is a digital currency that is created and managed through the use of advanced encryption methods and techniques known as cryptography.

The history of cryptocurrency has been studied in greater detail within the chapters above.

Digital currencies were a major part of academic research and study, before they finally made the jump to become actualized in the real world. Bitcoin was the first of all digital currencies to be launched, when it was introduced in the market in 2009.

The exponential rise and growth of crypto currencies opens doors to the conversation regarding their future. Will digital currencies ever be as popular and as ubiquitous as some of the fiat models currently operating in the market, or would they just dissipate into thin air, as quickly as they first made their mark?

Some of the things you can expect in the future with crypto currencies include:

The Economic Bull Run for United States Will End

As of today, the United States economy is currently experiencing its longest bull run in history. However, as the famous saying goes 'what goes up, must come down'. The United States' economy saw a successful bull run with plenty of success over an elongated period of time; however that Bull Run will soon end as the dollar will be replaced by more up to date crypto models.

The United States dollar enjoyed a decent run at the pinnacle of the forex market. However, the good times for the American market are about to come to an end soon. Whenever that happens, the blockchain will spring up as a potential source for investors to invest in.

The International Monetary Fund has also discussed the rise of a bear market for the United States dollar, and it is only a question of when and how.

Crypto currencies are already posing as potential alternatives for fiat currencies in the time of an inevitable market correction. The untethered nature of crypto coins will eventually maintain their value in the face of an economic struggle. When people see the value of all their fiat currencies falling, they'd be tempted and lured towards investing in the market for cryptos and digital currencies.

An Increase in Automation

Crypto currencies are further expected to infiltrate the public's consciousness. With the passage of time,cryptocurrencies would become a norm and would lead to increased automation in transactions.

We already know that cryptocurrencies make it extremely simple and easy for you to transfer money into an international account. Such international transfers were a pain to handle back in the day, but have been made a lot easier today with the use and widespread implementation of cryptocurrencies.

This ease of access and automation will further improve during the time to come, until we reach a time when digital currencies would be synonymous to perfect automation.

More Regulations

The future of digital currencies and crypto currencies will be met with advanced regulations and a stricter eye on the security and sanctity of these payment options. Lack of regulations has always been a pain point for the digital currencies industry. The market is currently full to the core with different options, but regulations are scarce, which is why security is a major issue for producers.

With countries looking to push their economies on the crypto bandwagon, it is a given fact that regulations will become more organized, and the entire crypto industry will become regulated.

Countries like Russia and even the United States have discussed the prospects of pushing their fiat currencies online and creating an amalgam with the digital world. These tactics can prove to be successful if implemented with care and precaution.

New Currencies and ICO

You can count the number of successful digital currencies on your finger tips. Bitcoin and Ethereal seem to be the more prominent ones, while others like Bitcoin Cash, Ripple and EOS follow closely behind.

However, the future of crypto and digital currencies is supposed to be even more fortunate for new currencies. IPOs could become a norm anytime, and digital currencies will be more easily and readily set for launch.

With a more feasible and regulated market, user interest in digital currencies will rise, leading to more profitable waters for new currencies to start their business.

Increased Scrutiny

The main benefits offered by Bitcoin and other digital currencies include increased decentralization and anonymity in transactions. While this has a ton of benefits, it has also proved to favor swindlers looking to partake in activities such as illegal laundering, drug peddling, weapons procurement and smuggling.

These features have attracted attention from the FED on more than one instance, as the FED is looking to put a hold on these activities.

What this means for digital currencies is that increased scrutiny is on the cards during the future. Increased scrutiny would help reduce the anonymity of transactions and those partaking in them, but would limit swindling and illegal activities being made possible through the platform.

Greater Acceptance

While the number of traders and merchants who accept payment in the form of digital currencies has slowly increased, these merchants are still in the minority. If digital currencies are to grow in the near future, it is important for them to achieve greater acceptance in the eyes of merchants and traders.

Consumers will start using the setup once they know they can use their reserves present on digital currency platforms for payments to all kinds of vendors and services.

The market cap and financial growth of digital currencies in the future cannot be predicted through a number, but what we do know is that enhanced growth is on the cards.

Chapter 4

Staying Safe in the Digital World of Tomorrow

This chapter discusses financial safety tips for staying safe in the digital world of tomorrow. Tips for consumers and businesses!

While all investments are risky in one way or the other, experts believe that investing in crypto currencies will be risky until widespread regulations and methods of scrutiny are implemented. Keeping this in mind it is necessary that you know and follow self-security tips for the future of finance.

Digital currency will be a big part of the economy in the future, and as a consumer you shall avoid all swindlers through these safety tips:

Use Secure Wallets

Online wallets act as a source to safeguard and protect your digital currency online. They carry all the rudimentary functions of a conventional bank, without any major plans or investment returns. Wallets can hold your digital assets, and allow you to perform periodic transactions using them.

As a consumer with digital currency assets, you should look to only invest in secure wallets you can trust. Some of the wallets coming from less reputable companies and sources happen to be malware in disguise and can sweep away your assets.

The best way out is to do some research before selecting the wallet you secure your digital assets in. An hour or two of research can tell you what you need to know about wallets that are safe and those that aren't.

Never Keep All Your Eggs in the Same Basket

This is one piece of advice you can follow in all kinds of investment, and not just crypto currencies. As an investor, it best suits you to diversify your portfolio by investing in different crypto currencies and not just one. For instance, you should buy some Bitcoins, a few coins of Ethereal and some other coins of Ripple or Bitcoin Cash. With a diversified portfolio, you can rest assured knowing that any major decrease in one currency wouldn't sweep you off your feet.

Similarly, you are better suited by placing your digital assets in more than one wallet, and not just one specific wallet. This will also safeguard your investments and wouldn't risk your digital standing.

Prepare for Volatility

Volatility is a major part and parcel of crypto markets. While this volatility might settle down with greater regulations and scrutiny, you need to be mentally prepared for what's to come. There are many investors who jumped on the Bitcoin band wagon when the crypto hit $18,000 back in 2017. However, sudden decreases meant Bitcoin was back at $9,000 in no time. This was a massive loss for some investors. However, there are use cases of other investors who made a fortune out of investments in crypto currencies as well.

Crypto currency is and will be the rage, but remember that successful investments come with patience and stability. If you can't handle the ups and downs of a volatile investment, then crypto currencies aren't meant for you.

Use Trusted Networks

Since the crypto market is purely online, you would want to mend your internet usage habits as well. As a beginner's tip, you should never perform a crypto or digital transaction on a public Wi-Fi or hotspot. Make sure you perform transactions through your own private network when money is involved. This would eventually safeguard your interests and would also make sure that no one can jump in and redirect your funds somewhere else.

Do not Discuss Investments

Keep all information related to your accounts and investments private. Cyber criminals are scouring social media and other online places to find targets openly discussing their digital investments.

It is best to remain quiet about all your investments in crypto currencies. Only share it with someone you trust and don't go beating your drums needlessly.

Conduct Smaller Trades

Finally, you should look to perform smaller trades, then performing one large trade. Performing a large trade can put you on the radar for a swindler targeting rich people. Even if you do have to perform a big trade, try breaking it down into smaller portions and proceed forward accordingly. Make yourself look like a small fish, so that swindlers and possible fraudsters aren't attracted to you. Also read up on possible digital currency scams so that you stray safe from them.

Keeping your financial safety intact within the future of crypto currencies would be complex, but can be handled with due care and precaution. The tips above will help prepare you for what is to come.

Blockchain Technology

Next edition coming soon!